故 宫 博 物 院
Palace Museum

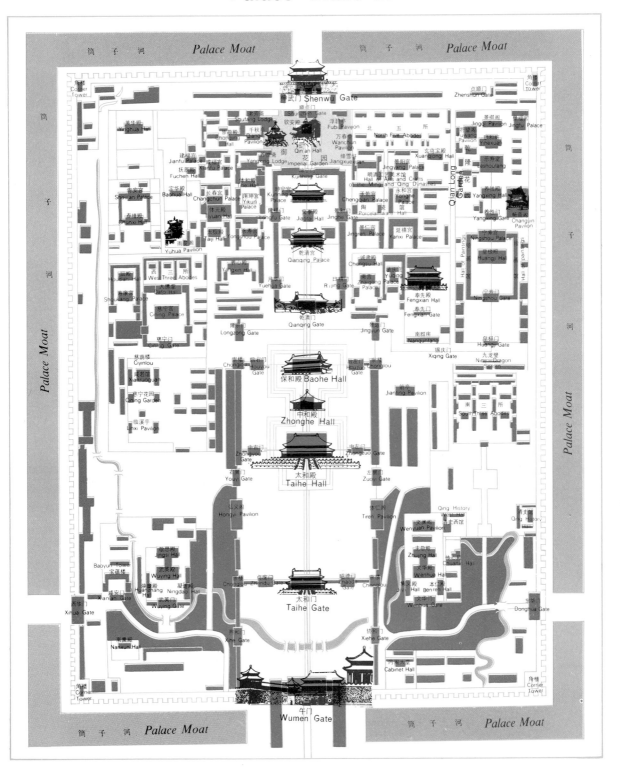

The Former Imperial Palace in Beijing

中国世界语出版社　北京

CHINA ESPERANTO PRESS, BEIJING, CHINA

Fouy edition :June 2000

Published by China Esperanto Press, Beijing, China
Printed in China
Distributed by China International Book Trading
Corporation (Guojishudian)
35 W. Chegongzhuang Xilu, Beijing, China
P.O. Box 399, Post code: 100044
ISBN 7-5052-0263-4
06000
85-CE-461P

目　录
CONTENTS

紫禁城——中国最大的皇宫

故宫又称紫禁城，是中国明（公元1368—1644年）、清（公元1616—1911年）两朝皇宫，曾有24个皇帝在此处理朝政和居住。

故宫以其悠久的历史，宏大的规模和独具特色的建筑艺术享誉世界。

故宫的建造始于明初。明朝开国皇帝朱元璋（公元1368—1398年在位）于1368年在应天府（今江苏省南京市）即位称帝，建号大明，改元洪武。洪武三年，朱元璋封皇四子朱棣为燕王，镇守北平。洪武三十一年朱元璋卒于南京，皇长孙朱允炆继位，是为建文帝。新帝为加强中央集权，采取"削藩"政策，此举激怒了实力雄厚的燕王。朱棣以"靖难"为名，发动了历时四年的"靖难之役"，攻陷南京，登上了帝位，改年号为"永乐"。

永乐元年（1403年）正月，朱棣将北平升为陪都，改称北京。翌年，下诏营建北京宫苑，并抽调大批官员、军士、工匠、民夫，分头采木烧砖，整治地基。至永乐十八年，紫禁城告成。这一规模宏大的宫殿建筑群座落在北京城的南北中轴线上，占地72万平方米，共有房舍号称9999间半（现存8000余间），约15万平方米，是中国迄今保存最完整的帝王宫阙。

为修建这座巨大的"城中之城"，明王朝倾全国人力物力，征集能工巧匠10万余名，民夫逾百万。所用建筑材料采自全国各地，木料采自湖广、江西、山西等省；汉白玉石出自北京房山县；墁地金砖烧制于苏州；砌墙用砖来自山东临清。真可谓"量中华之物力，给予人间之仙阙"，堪称中国古代宫殿建筑之最。

紫禁城的建筑布局分外朝、内廷两部分。外朝以太和、中和、保和三大殿为主体，左右衔连文华、武英两殿。三大殿以北为内廷，内廷又分中、东、西三路。中为乾清宫、交泰殿、坤宁宫，其后是御花园；中路两侧为东、西六宫。东六宫向南是奉先殿、斋宫、南三所，西六宫往南为养心殿。内廷外围东有宁寿全宫，西有慈宁、寿安诸宫。这种布局，充分体现了古礼所谓"前朝后寝"格局，前朝为"大内正衙"，后寝即所谓"三宫六院"。

如此恢宏浩繁的建筑群，所以未给人纷杂之感，主要因为在建筑手法上突出了一条极为明显的中轴线。它南起永定门，北至钟鼓楼，全长8公里，皇家禁苑部分约占1/3。整个紫禁城的建筑物以中轴线为中心展开，天安门为其序幕，外朝三大殿形成高潮，景山为终曲。整个建筑群体主从分明，跌宕起伏，前后呼应，左右对称，由此形成紫禁城乃至整个北京城的雄伟气魄和井然秩序。

中轴线两边，还伸出了几条次轴线；左有文华——东六宫轴线，右有武英——西六宫轴线，两边又分列宁寿全宫、慈宁诸宫。渐次连接的五条轴线宛如五根金线，将紫禁城纷繁复杂的诸多庭院贯连成五串珍珠，撒在北京城中心，璀璨夺目。

紫禁城作为中国古代建筑的代表作，在艺术处理上有鲜明特点。主要表现在建筑大师们善于将建筑物的各种构件进行艺术加工，从而使构件本身既有实用功能，又有美化建筑物的装饰作用，这突出地表现在紫禁城的屋顶上。中国古建筑的屋顶，由于木结构的缘故，形体显得庞大浑厚，为造好大屋顶，聪明的工匠们巧妙地利用木质建筑材料的特点，将整个屋顶做成曲面形，从屋檐到屋的四角都微微翘起，观之如巨鹏展翅，大雁凌云。在长期实践中，中国匠人又创造了庑殿、歇山、攒尖等屋顶形式（见以下各

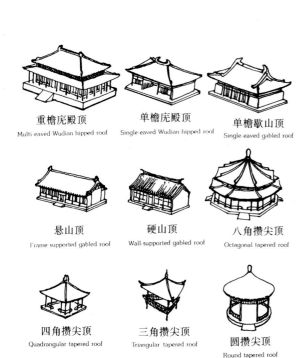

重檐庑殿顶
Multi-eaved Wudian hipped roof

单檐庑殿顶
Single-eaved Wudian hipped roof

单檐歇山顶
Single-eaved gabled roof

悬山顶
Frame-supported gabled roof

硬山顶
Wall-supported gabled roof

八角攒尖顶
Octagonal tapered roof

四角攒尖顶
Quadrangular tapered roof

三角攒尖顶
Triangular tapered roof

圆攒尖顶
Round tapered roof

盝顶
Tier-eaved roof

卷棚顶
Curved-canopy roof

扇面殿顶
Fan-shaped roof

图），以及各种形式交叉组合的复杂形态，如紫禁城角楼，就是这种复杂形态的典型代表。特别值得一提的是，紫禁城殿亭楼阁的屋脊和飞檐上的压脊构件被加工成形态各异的神兽和仙人，它们各自不仅有特定的寓意，而且数量的多寡是建筑物等级的标志。这些外表看似装饰性的构件，还具有必不可少的实用功能。正是由于建筑师们在建造屋顶时从整体到局部都作了艺术加工，突出了民族特色，从而使屋顶成为中国古建筑的主要特征之一，并为世界建筑业在建造同类建筑物时提供了摹仿的范式。

中国古建筑的另一特征，表现为建筑工匠

们不但敢于而且善于巧妙设色，他们利用颜色的强烈反差使建筑物主体突出，层次分明。紫禁城宫殿，远望如金波荡漾的浩瀚之海。它以黄绿色为主调，顶盖为黄色琉璃瓦，下饰青绿为主调的彩画，殿身为红墙、红柱、红门窗，底为汉白玉石台基，殿内地面多为绛色。如此大胆地将黄与兰、红与绿、白与黑放在一起，产生了强烈的色彩对比效果。这一传统的设色手法与某些绘画流派所称道的色彩柔和、含而不露大相径庭，使建筑物颜色的主调鲜明突出，辅调策应生辉，给人以清心爽目之感。

紫禁城的室内装饰和陈设也别具特色。人们巧妙地利用房屋内部结构、装饰与室内家具、珍宝、字画等物融为一体，用结构与装饰的精美反衬陈设的珍奇与华贵，反之亦然，二者互为表里，相得益彰。在客观上给人的感觉是，无论走进一所殿堂或迈入一方居室，仿佛都是在艺术陈列室中徜徉。如清康乾时代（十七世纪中叶至十八世纪上半叶）的木制家具，以其用料讲究、制作精良、雕刻华美著称于世，成为中国木制家具一绝。精美的家具与室内古香古色的屏风、隔断、博古架相配，即使斗室也不会给人以局促之感，反而使人觉得室内空间宽敞、纵深有序。至于紫禁城的主要殿堂，由于天花板均为大面积的沥粉贴金彩画，天花板正中又有雕刻精妙的金龙藻井，再加上阔门、敞窗、金砖殿面互相辉映，尤显得开阔明亮，恢宏庄严。

无论是宫阙还是亭榭，本是一种物质架构，但深层次地反映了特定历史时期的文化内涵和文明程度。封建王朝的宫苑以其相沿成制的定式表现出封建王朝的礼制秩序、政治规范和伦理精神，其中需要突出表现的是皇权至高无上的尊严。作为皇宫建筑师们必须从整体布局、规模乃至具体形式、色彩、装饰、陈设诸多方面用一种直观的能充分体现集权政治和森严等级的形式特征表现出最高统治者的精神内涵。正是在这一点上,紫禁城以其精绝神幻的建筑形式,给人一种皇权至上、辉煌绝伦的精神感受。

这突出表现在代表皇权的主要建筑物集中于中轴线,其中太和殿为重中之重,它巍然座落于前朝的中心位置。这里是皇家政治活动的中心,皇帝即位、大婚、朝会、赐宴以及命将出征和殿试均在这里举行,所以它的体量最大,等级最高,充分体现了皇权第一的思想。其他如中和、保和殿虽然也是皇帝频繁活动的场所,但它们毕竟不是重大活动的中心,所以它们的建筑规模、豪华程度明显逊于太和殿,表现出严格的等级区别。以垂脊兽为例,太和殿设置十尊,且兽体硕大,保和殿设置九尊,中和殿仅七尊;而中轴线两侧的东西六宫主殿仅设置五尊。由此不难看出,紫禁城内人与人之间复杂的等级关系,即封建社会的等级制度,在这里被明白无误的建筑形式完整地体现出来了。等级是权力的象征,也是皇权赖以维系的基础,这其中礼制与政治的内涵却被我们聪明的古代匠人以简洁明快的物质架构昭示于世人。

最值得一提、也是令今人叹服的是,紫禁城的表象特征将中国古代神秘的哲学观念完整地传达给世人,它的成组或单体建筑无论是方位、朝向、形体或装饰都有特定的含义,绝非随意而置,恣肆拼凑,而是按照古已有之特定的观念组合而成的。

阴阳五行哲学观念在中国流行了近3000年。所谓阴阳,初指日光的向背,向日为阳,背日为阴。后来,古代思想家用这个概念来解释自然现象,提出"一阴一阳谓之道",把阴阳交替看作宇宙的根本规律,并以此比附社会现象,引申为上下、君民、君臣关系等等。所谓五行,系指水、火、木、金、土五种物质,古代思想家认为,它们是构成万物的基本元素。五行之间"相生相克",相生意味着相互促进,如"木生火,火生土,土生金,金生水,水生木"等;相克意味着相互排斥,如"水胜火,火胜金,金胜木,木胜土,土胜水"等。这些观点具有朴素的唯物论和自发的辩证法因素。

按照上述观念,外朝为皇帝活动的主要场所,皇帝为阳,从火主大,故作施政场所;后寝为帝后颐养寝卧之地,皇后为阴,从水主藏,故作寝居之处。中轴线以东,多为文治宫殿,从木主春;以西,属兵刑、武备要地,从金主秋。据此,文华殿为讲经习文之所,居东;武英殿为设谋谈武之地,座西,一文一武拱卫着中央三大殿。不仅如此,数字也有阴阳之分,奇数为阳,偶数为阴,所以屋脊兽多为奇数。奇数中以九为尊,所以故宫大门(除东华门)均用九行九排门钉;皇家器物多以九件陈列,以示皇权至尊至贵,天下无双。

毫不夸张地说,阴阳五行学说渗透到紫禁城各个角落,成为建筑工匠们施工的指导原则。

紫禁城以其完美的古代建筑艺术、丰富的文化精神内涵而成为中国古代文明的象征。在这里,还藏有大量的历史文物和艺术品,其中有许多是稀世绝宝。1925年紫禁城改名为故宫博物院。新中国成立后,中国政府每年拨巨款对它进行保护和维修。现在的故宫,已成为中国最负盛名的旅游热点。

The Forbidden City — Former Imperial Palace

The former Imperial Palace, also known as the Forbidden City, was the residence to 24 emperors of the Ming and Qing dynasties from 1420 to 1911. Now it is open as the Palace Museum.

Zhu Yuanzhang founded the Ming Dynasty in 1368 and made Nanjing his capital. He made his fourth son Zhu Di the Prince of Yan and commander of Beijing garrison. Zhu Yuanzhang died in 1398. His grandson Zhu Yunwen succeeded him. The new emperor wanted to reduce the power of local garrison commanders. Zhu Di, enraged, staged a revolt and usurped the throne from his nephew. He decided to move the capital to Beijing.

In 1406 Emperor Yong Le (Zhu Di) ordered the construction of the palace in Beijing. A hundred thousand artisans and a million workmen were conscripted on the project. Wood were sent from southern provinces, marble cut at Fangshan in Beijing's outskirts, bricks for paving the ground baked in Suzhou, Jiangsu Province, and bricks for the walls made in Linqing, Shandong Province. The new palace was completed in 1420.

The Imperial Palace is composed of the Outer Court and the Inner Court. In the Outer Court along a single axis are the three main halls: the Hall of Supreme Harmony (Taihedian), the Hall of Central Harmony (Zhonghedian), and the Hall of Preserving Harmony (Baohedian). On either side of them are two minor halls: the Hall of Literary Glory (Wenhuadian), and the Hall of the Martial Spirit (Wuyingdian).

The buildings in the Inner Court are arranged along three routes. On the central line are the three main halls: the Palace of Heavenly Purity (Qianqinggong), the Hall of Union (Jiaotaidian) and the Palace of Earthly Tranquility (Kunninggong). At the northern end of this line is the Imperial Garden. Parallel to the central line are the Six Western Palaces and the Six Eastern Palaces. To the south of the Six Eastern Palaces are the Hall of Worshipping Ancesters (Fengxiandian), the Palace of Abstinency (Zhaigong) and Nansansu; to the south of the Six Western Palaces is the Hall of Mental Cultivation (Yangxindian). On the eastern side of the three main halls is the Palace of Tranquil Longevity (Ningshougong); on the western side are the Palace of Motherly Tranquility (Cininggong) and the Palace of Longevity and Peace (Shou'angong).

The entire palace area, rectangular in shape and 720,000 square meters in size, takes up one-third of the 8-kilometer-long central axis of the old Beijing city from the city gate of Yongdingmen on the south to the Drum and Bell Towers on the north. This harmonious assemblage of buildings displays the best characteristics of Chinese architecture — majestic style, flawless construction, fine coordination of the whole and the parts.

Most of ancient buildings in China have large wooden roofs with upturned eaves. They fall in several types such as Wudian hipped roof, gabled roof and capered roof (see pictures). A representative masterpiece is the Corner Tower at each of the four corners of the Imperial Palace. The zoomorphic ornaments (liwen) on the roof ridges in the palace deserve particular mention. They are in the shapes of divine animals and immortals. Their number on the roof ridge is decided by the importance of the building — the more important a building the larger is the number. Another feature of the Imperial Palace is the bold application of colors. The dominant colors are yellow and dark green: yellow glazed roof tiles and large stretches of dark green in the ornamental painting. The walls, pillars and windows are painted vermilion. The halls stand on white marble terraces. Such sharp color contrast is against the usual concept that colors should be combined on a graduation basis.

The furniture, treasures and works of painting and calligraphy are arranged to merge with the interior as a whole. One feels entering an art display in every building. The wooden furniture such as treasure shelves, partition screens and tables and chairs made during the reign of Emperor Kang Xi of the Qing Dynasty from the mid-17th to the early 18th century in the Imperial Palace are masterpieces. They are famous for their elaborate carvings and meticulous workmanship. With all these furniture in the room one does not feel crowded. The gilded ceiling and the coffered ceiling in the center, wide doors, large windows and golden paved floor make the main halls in the Imperial Palace seem more spacious than they actually are.

The Imperial Palace represented the supreme power of the emperor and strict hierarchy of feudal China. The size, layout, color, ornaments and interior decoration of a building were decided by its political and spiritual status. The imperial authority was well displayed by the buildings on the central axis. The Hall of Supreme Harmony, the center of the emperor's activities, is located in the middle of the Outer Court. This is where grand ceremonies were held, such as the accession of a new emperor to the throne,

the emperor's birthday, or the pronouncement of important edicts. On each of its roof ridges there are 10 zoomorphic ornamental animals, the largest number allowed, and their size is much larger than those on other buildings. The Hall of Preserving Harmony has nine, the Hall of Central Harmony has seven, and the main halls in the Six Eastern Palaces and Six Western Palaces have only five.

The construction of the Imperial Palace followed strictly the mythological philosophy of ancient China. The direction, shape and ornamentation of each group of buildings or individual buildings all bear certain significance. According to the ancient philosophy, the universe is made of the *Yin* and *Yang* and five elements (metal, wood, water, fire and earth). Such belief is 3,000 years old in China. The emperor belonged to *yang* (male), so he ruled the country from the Outer Court. The empress belonged to *yin* (female), so she stayed in the Inner Court. According to the philosophy odd numbers belong to *yang* while even numbers belong to *yin*. The number of most zoomorphic ornaments in the Imperial Palace is odd. And it also believes nine is the highest number. So ornamental objects, even the door knobs in the Imperial Palace are in the number of nine to symbolize the highest authority of the emperor.

The former Imperial Palace keeps a great quantity of historic relics and artistic objects. In 1925 it was turned into a museum. Since the founding of the People's Republic in 1949 the central government has repaired and renovated it on several occasions. It allots large sums every year for its maintenance. Now it is a hot tourist attraction in China.

中轴线区

中轴线区是故宫最主要的部分,它包括前三殿和后三宫。前三殿分别为太和殿、中和殿、保和殿,是皇帝从事政务活动的主要场所;后三宫包括乾清宫、交泰殿和坤宁宫,是皇帝居寝和憩息之所。

中轴线建筑以高大、宏阔、豪华为特征,以表现皇家宫殿的至尊至贵以及皇权统治的绝对权威。

Along the Central Axis

The former Imperial Palace is divided into the Outer Court and Inner Court. Along the central axis are the three major imperial halls and three inner palaces. The emperor conducted state affairs in the three major halls, Taihe, Zhonghe and Baohe, while the three inner palaces, Qianqing, Jiaotai and Kunning served as living quarters of the emperor and his consorts.

All the structures along the central axis are grand and magnificent, symbolizing the supreme power of the imperial rule.

故宫远眺

Bird's-eye view of the Palace.

天安门 原为皇城正门,建于明永乐十五年(1417 年),初名承天门。此门重楼九楹,高 33.7 米,称天安门,取皇帝"受命于天,安邦治民"之意。新中国成立后,天安门已成为中华人民共和国的象征。

Gate of Heavenly Peace (Tian'anmen) Tian'anmen was the front gate of the Imperial Palace during the Ming and Qing dynasties. Originally built in 1417 and named Chengtianmen, it was burnt down and rebuilt several times. The present gate tower, 33.7 meters high and with five openings, was rebuilt in 1651 and renamed Tian'anmen (Gate of Heavenly Peace). The imposing tower today is a symbol of the People's Republic of China.

华表 天安门前后各立华表一对。中国的华表起源甚早,初为木制,为纳谏而设,后发展成路标,称华表。现在的华表已无原意,只起装饰作用。其顶端蹲兽叫"犼",为古人想象中的神兽。天安门后华表犼头朝里,寓意皇帝不要沉缅于宫廷宴乐,应常出宫体惜民情,故叫"望君出";前华表犼头朝外,提醒皇帝不要迷恋山水,应回朝勤政,因而叫"望君归"。

Huabiao Before and behind the Gate of Heavenly Peace stand two pairs of sculpted white marble columns called huabiao. The original purpose to erect wooden poles was for the ruler to solicit complaints from the common people. It eventually became a land mark and finally an ornamental object. The squatting mythical animal at the top of each huabiao in front of Tian'anmen is called "hou". It faces south. The legend says it kept an eye on the emperor while he was on an inspection tour and reminded him to return to the capital to attend to state affairs.

角楼　故宫城墙四隅各设角楼一座，它们均为六个歇山顶组合而成的奇特整体。每楼三层屋檐设计有 28 个翼角，72 条屋脊，造型精巧玲珑，堪称中国古建一绝。

Corner Tower　At each of the four corners of the Palace stands a unique tower, each with six hipped and gabled roofs. The three-tiered eaves sloping into 28 upturning curves, together with 10 gables and 72 ridges, add much grace to the structure.

午门 位于天安门北、端门后,它座落于京城南北中轴线上,居中向阳,位当子午,故名午门。城台上建崇楼五座,俗称"五凤楼"。门为五洞,中门供皇帝出入,叫"御路";王公大臣走左右门;掖门平时不开,唯殿试时,文武进士按单双号分进左右掖门。

Meridian Gate (Wumen)   It is the largest gate of the Palace and stands on the central axis of Beijing City. Surmounted by five pavilions, this massive gate is also known as the "Five-Phoenix Tower". The gate has five openings. The central one was used exclusively by the emperor. Court officials passed through the two gates near the central one. The two sidegates were opened only to let in successful candidates of imperial examinations.

午门余晖　　Sunset over Meridian Gate.

内金水河　源于北京西郊玉泉山,从故宫西北角地沟流入宫中,河道弯弯曲曲,水碧似玉,故又名玉带河。

Inner Golden Water River　Fed by spring water from Yuquan Hill on the western outskirts of Beijing, the canal runs from northwestern corner and through the Palace. It is also called "Jade Belt River" for its clear water of emerald color.

内金水桥 内金水河上横跨雕栏玉砌石桥五座,桥因河
得名。

Inner Golden Water Bridge Five white marble bridges
are built over the Inner Golden Water River.

弘义阁　为太和殿前西庑,原是明代珍藏《永乐大典》的处所。阁为三层九楹,一、二层间为暗层,这是中国古建筑中阁的特点,也是楼与阁的区别之一。

Spreading Righteous Tower (Hongyige)　The *Grand Yongle Dictionary* was originally kept here. The tower has three stories but the first and second floors cannot be seen from the outside. So it appears as a two-story structure.

太和门 为宫中等级最高的门,是外朝三大殿的正门。明、清两朝均有"御门听政"之制,清康熙帝(1661—1722 年在位)以前的皇帝均设座于此听政。

Gate of Supreme Harmony (Taihemen)
This main entrance to the Outer Court is the tallest of all gates in the Palace. Before the reign of Emperor Kang Xi (1661-1722) it served the emperor as a reception hall for ministers.

太和门望楼　其上遍绘彩画。中国的彩画是从木结构建筑上的涂料发展而成的，既可防腐，又有装饰作用。彩画分和玺彩画、旋子彩画和苏式彩画三个等级，和玺彩画为宫廷专用，其特点是，以龙凤为主要图案，间补以花卉，并大面积沥粉贴金，给人以金碧辉煌、雍容华贵之感。

Tower of the Gate of Supreme Harmony　The tower is painted with colorful lacquer. The main designs are dragons and phoenixes amidst flowering plants. Large stretches are gold painted to show imperial extravagance.

铜狮 太和门前左右两侧各设铜狮一尊,左雄右雌,威武凶悍。雄狮右足踏绣球,象征权力和一统天下,雌狮左足抚幼狮,象征子嗣昌盛。

Bronze Lions Two bronze lions are placed at either side of the Gate of Supreme Harmony. The one on the west side is female with a baby lion under its left paw, symbolizing fertility of the royal family; the one on the east is male with an embroidered ball under its right paw, symbolizing the imperial power.

石亭 设置于太和门前东侧,内储嘉量。嘉量是中国古代的标准量器,上部为斛,下部为斗,左耳为升,右耳为合、龠。

Stone Pavilion The small marble pavilion in front of the Gate of Supreme Harmony keeps a Jia Liang (Grain Measure), used in ancient China. It is made of bronze and then gilded.

俯瞰外朝三大殿 这里是故宫的核心建筑,三大殿座落
于三层重叠的"工"字形丹陛之上,威严壮观,气势非凡。

Bird's-eye view of the three main halls The imposing
imperial halls stand on a three-tiered marble terrace. They
are the main part of the Imperial Palace.

石匣 置于太和门前西侧，匣为大理石制成，匣盖以盘龙为纽，内储米谷、五色线，寓意年丰政和。

Stone Casket A marble casket is placed to the right of the Gate of Supreme Harmony. A coiling dragon is engraved on the lid. Grain used to be put inside the casket to betoken good harvest.

丹陛 为汉白玉石雕砌而成，共三层，通高8.13米。每层丹陛均横卧地袱，绕以汉白玉石栏杆，上立望柱1458根，柱头精雕云龙云凤图案。地袱下设排水沟，沟口雕制螭蝮头1142个。每至雨天，千龙喷水，蔚为壮观。

Danbi (Imperial Terrace) The three main halls of the Palace stand on a vast three-tiered marble terrace which is 8.13 meters high and edged with 1,458 white marble balusters carved with patterns of dragons and phoenixes. At the base of these balustrades are 1,142 gargoyles in the shape of dragon head which make a spectacle during a downpour.

螭蝮 是中国民间传说中类似龙的神兽。传说龙生九子，螭蝮为第六子，性好水，故多立于桥柱或设置于排水沟口。图中螭蝮既可排水，又有装饰作用。

Paxia According to Chinese mythology, the dragon has nine sons. Paxia is the sixth son. It loves water. So its image is often seen at a water outlet.

太和殿广场 占地三万多平方米,正中为巨石铺成的 "御路",其左右为磨砖对缝的"海墁"砖地。每逢大典, 御道两侧设置铜制品级山,文东武西,诸大臣依官阶跪 于品级山旁;各国使臣亦按指定位置跪拜。

Square of the Hall of Supreme Harmony The open ground in front of the Hall of Supreme Harmony covers more than 30,000 square meters. The central "Imperial Road" is paved with large stone slabs and the rest with bricks. On major occasions, bronze markers were placed along the sides of the "Imperial Road" and court officials knelt in the order of ranks. Foreign envoys knelt at their designated spot.

太和殿　俗称金銮殿，建于1420年。大殿面阔十一间，进深五间，重檐庑殿顶，通高35.5米，总面积2300平方米。殿内横竖梁枋182根，内外大柱84根。此殿是中国现存最大的木构殿。明、清两代皇帝即位、大婚、朝会以及元旦赐宴、命将出征和殿试进士等，均在此举行。

Hall of Supreme Harmony (Taihedian)　Commonly known as the Hall of Gold Throne, the magnificent structure was built in 1420. It is 35.5 meters high and has a floor space of 2,300 square meters with 182 beams and 84 pillars. It is the largest wood structure extant in China. During the Ming and Qing dyansties grand ceremonies such as the enthronement of the emperor, New Year's Day, proclamation of imperial edicts, receiving successful candidates of imperial examination, appointment of commander-in-chief of expedition troops were held here.

太和殿雪景　　Snow shrouded Hall of Supreme Harmony.

螭吻　设置于太和殿正脊两端,由十三块琉璃件构成,总高3.4米,重4.3吨。它是中国最大的螭吻。

Dragon Head Chiwen　At either end of the roof ridge of the Hall of Supreme Harmony is a dragon head. The largest roof ornament in China is 3.4 meters high, weighs 4.3 tons and is composed of 13 glazed tiles.

垂脊兽 为中国古建筑垂脊上的饰物,多以神话中的吉祥兽为形象,其数目的多寡,取决于殿宇等级的高低。太和殿为殿宇之最,所以设置十尊,它们分别是龙、凤、狮、天马、海马、狻猊、押鱼、獬豸、斗牛、行什;它们的前面为"骑凤仙人"。

Roof Animal Ornaments Animal ornaments are often seen at the end of roof ridges of ancient buildings in China. The number varies according to the importance of the building. The Hall of Supreme Harmony, as the most important hall of the Imperial Palace, has ten mythical animals on the roof: dragon, phoenix, lion, heavenly horse, sea horse, suanni, xiayu, xiezhi, divine bull and xingshi, preceded by an immortal riding a phoenix.

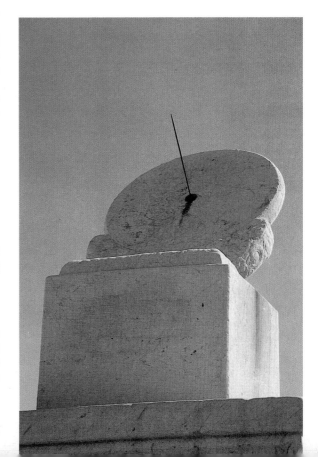

日晷 是中国古代利用日影测定时间的仪器,故宫的日晷分别安放于太和殿、午门、乾清宫和皇极殿前,既为计时,也象征皇帝一统授时。

Sundial In ancient times people used a sundial to show the time of the day from the shadow cast by an upright pin on a dial. Sundials are placed at the Hall of Supreme Harmony, Meridian Gate, Palace of Heavenly Purity and Hall of Imperial Supremacy.

铜龟 龟为长寿的象征。太和殿前陈设铜龟寓意延年益寿。每逢大典,龟中升起袅袅香烟,缭绕宫殿,一派神秘气氛。

Bronze Tortoise The bronze tortoises are symbols of long life. In the old days during a grand ceremony, sandalwood was burnt inside the hollow belly of the tortoises which poured forth coiling smoke around the hall so as to create a mysterious and solemn atmosphere.

铜鹤 中国素有"鹤寿千年"之说。太和殿前的铜鹤寓意天子福寿万年,长生不老。

Bronze Crane Bronze cranes also symbolize longevity. The one in front of the Hall of Supreme Harmony was to wish a long life of the emperor.

鼎式香炉 太和殿三层丹陛上共有18个鼎式香炉,代表当时朝廷管辖的18个省。每逢大典,炉内点燃檀香和藏香,青烟缭绕,香气袭人。

Ding-style Incense Burner There are 18 bronze incense burners on the three-tiered marble terrace of the Hall of Supreme Harmony, representing 18 provinces of Imperial China. On major occasions sandalwood and Tibetan incense were burnt in them.

太和殿内景 殿内陈设如当年帝、后临朝状。正中为七级高台的地平床，上设屏风、宝座、御案，两侧为宫扇、珐琅塔和仙鹤。殿内金碧辉煌，庄严华贵。

Inside the Hall of Supreme Harmony

The interior of the Gold Throne Hall is preserved as in ancient times. On the raised platform is the gilded imperial throne placed on a dais two meters high. Behind the throne is a carved screen. On either side of the throne are a crane-shaped candlestick, an elephant-shaped incense burner and a column-shaped incense burner with a pagoda top which are all cloisonne wares.

宝座 为故宫诸多宝座之魁。宝座上半部为圈椅靠背，背上金龙缠绕，下部为金漆蟠龙须弥座，座后为七扇金龙屏风。据说袁世凯称帝时，宝座被搬走，辗转不知下落，1959 年在一家具库找到，经修复放置原位，一展当年风采。

Throne The painted golden throne with a splendid screen behind it stands on a two-meter high dais in the center of the Hall of Supreme Harmony. Its back and the lower part are covered with coiled dragons. Warlord Yuan Shikai moved it from the hall when he proclaimed himself emperor. In 1959 it was found in a used furniture store and restored to its original place.

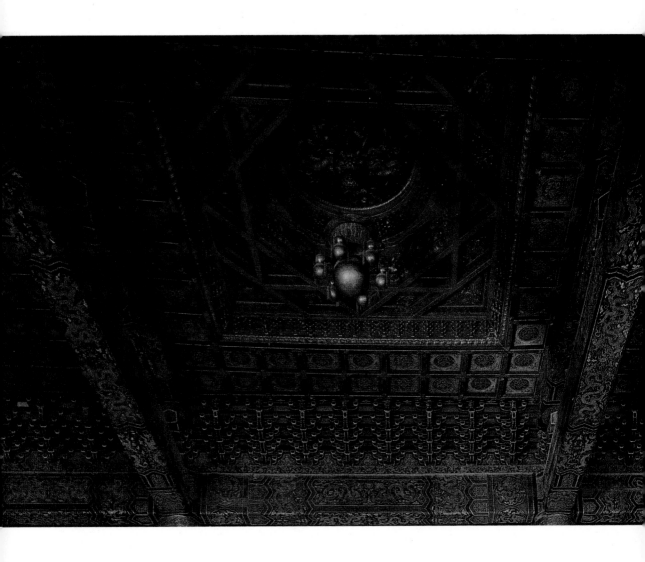

太和殿藻井 井内金龙盘卧，口衔轩辕镜，镜下为宝座，
以示中国皇帝皆为轩辕氏黄帝的正统继承者。传说袁
世凯登基时惧怕大圆球掉下砸头，曾将宝座后移。

Coffered Ceiling The gilded coffered ceiling high above
the throne is decorated with a dragon-phoenix pattern.
Hanging underneath are glass balls called "Mirrors of the
Yellow Emperor" which represent orthodox succession.
Warlord Yuan Shikai removed the balls because he was
afraid they might fall on his head.

大柱　整座大殿内外由 84 根巨柱支撑，殿内有 6 根通体遍饰金龙云山图案，金光闪烁，庄严华贵，使人叹为观止。

Gilded Columns　The Hall of Supreme Harmony is supported by 84 giant columns. The six columns inside are gilded and carved with coiled dragons amidst mountains and clouds.

龙柜 为紫檀木制作,陈于太和殿,柜门浮雕云龙,刀法深峻,磨工精细,为清代中期木家具精品。柜左为实榻门的垂花门楼,其质亦为紫檀木,造型美观,雕刻精致,虽为门楣,实为艺术佳作。

Dragon Cabinet The purple sandalwood cabinet in the Hall of Supreme Harmony bears elaborate relief carvings of dragons and clouds. It is a master piece of furniture of the mid Qing Dynasty. On its left is a door arch with open work carvings, also of purple sandalwood.

中和殿　位于太和殿后,为深广各五间的方形殿,其顶为单檐四角攒尖鎏金宝顶。此殿是皇帝去太和殿举行大典前稍事休息或演习礼仪的地方。

Hall of Middle Harmony (Zhonghedian)　The square hall with a pyramidic roof stands behind the Hall of Supreme Harmony. The emperor would take a rest before he went to the Hall of Supreme Harmony. He also practiced rites here.

中和殿内景 殿内安设地平床，上置宝座、屏风；床下殿
面立有金鼎和薰炉等。皇帝御殿时，薰炉升烟，气氛神
秘。

Inside the Hall of Middle Harmony The throne is placed
on a dais in front of a screen. When the emperor came to
the hall incense would be burnt in the burners which stand
at the foot of the dais.

肩輿　俗称轿子,是清代皇帝在宫内使用的交通工具。
此肩輿为乾隆年间(1736—1795 年)所造。

Sedan Chair　The emperor was carried on a sedan chair
to travel inside the Imperial Palace. This one was built
during the reign of Emperor Qian Long between 1736 and
1795.

保和殿 是外朝最后的大殿，面阔九间，深五间，寓意"九五之尊"。明朝皇帝曾在此册封皇后、太子。清朝皇帝在此宴请蒙古、新疆的王公大臣；乾隆皇帝以后，在此举行殿试，选拔贤才。

Hall of Preserving Harmony (Baohedian) The last of the three main halls in the Outer Court is nine bays wide and five bays deep. In the Ming Dynasty, before going to the ceremony of granting title on the empress or the crown prince, the emperor would change into full ceremonial dress in this hall. In the Qing Dynasty, the emperor gave banquet in honor of Uygur and Mongol nobles. From 1789 onward the final session of the Civil Service Examinations was held in this hall with the supervision of the emperor.

保和殿内景 殿内陈设与中和殿相似，仅形制有别。

Inside the Hall of Preserving Harmony The interior decoration is similar to that of the Hall of Middle Harmony.

云龙雕石 位于保和殿后，为宫内最大石雕。雕造于明代，清乾隆年间曾磨后重雕，总长 16.75 米，宽 3.07 米，重约 250 吨。石上精刻山崖、海水、祥云和九条游龙，形象极为生动。

Dragon-Cloud Jade Carving It is placed behind the Hall of Preserving Harmony. The largest carving in the Palace Museum was first made during the Ming Dynasty. It was recarved during the Qing Dynasty. It is 16.75 meters long and 3.07 meters wide. On it are exquisite designs of mountain cliffs, sea waves, clouds and nine dragons.

内廷鸟瞰   Bird's-eye view of the Inner Court.

乾清门　为内廷正门。门为五楹大殿,三洞朱门设于后檐柱间。由于大殿宽阔宏丽,清代自康熙皇帝起,将太和门的"御门听政"改在此处。

Gate of Heavenly Purity (Qianqingmen)　The Gate of Heavenly Purity, built like a mansion, is the main entrance to the Inner Court. Beginning from Emperor Kang Xi, the Qing emperors sometimes gave audience to government officials at this gate.

海缸　为宫中防火而设,共有铜、铁缸 308 口,其中鎏金铜缸 18 口。逢大典则用黄布将海缸罩上,显得庄严肃穆。

Water Vats　There are altogether 308 water vats of bronze and iron in the Palace Museum. Eighteen of them are gilded. They were used to prevent fire. During grand ceremonies the vats were wrapped up with yellow cloth to add solemnity to the atmosphere.

军机处　位于乾清门内右门旁。1729 年清廷对西北用兵，为统一指挥而设军机处，在以后的演变中，此机构凌驾于内阁之上，成为中枢机构，至晚清，几可左右清廷政治。

Office of the Privy Council (Junjichu)　Located by the Inner Right Gate not far from the Gate of Heavenly Purity, the office was set up in 1729 by the Qing court to coordinate the war affairs in Northwest China. Eventually it became powerful enough to override the Inner Cabinet.

铜缸刮痕　鎏金铜缸每口鎏金百两。1900 年八国联军入侵北京，洗劫宫中珍宝时，缸上鎏金亦被刮剥，至今刀痕累累。

Gilded Bronze Vat　Each vat used 100 taels of gold to gild it. In 1900 the Allied Forces of the Eight Powers invaded Beijing and looted the Imperial Palace. Soldiers scraped the gold off the vats with their bayonets. Even today the scrapes are still clearly visible.

乾清宫 内廷正殿,宽九间,深五间,重檐庑殿顶,梁枋饰金龙和玺彩画,为内廷等级最高的殿。明、清两代皇帝以此为寝宫,并在此处理朝政。 皇帝驾崩,停灵柩于殿内。

Palace of Heavenly Purity (Qianqinggong) The double-eaved building rises 24 meters high and is decorated with minute paintings. It is the most important building in the Inner Court. During the Ming and Qing dynasties, it served as the living quarters of the emperor, who also attended state affairs here. The dead emperor was also laid in state in this palace.

老虎洞　为乾清宫丹陛下的石洞，是宫监们的通道，俗称"老虎洞"。明末天启皇帝（1620—1627 年在位）朱由校常于月夜率内侍潜匿洞中捉迷藏。

Tiger's Cave　Located under the marble terrace of the Hall of Heavenly Purity, it was a passageway for eunuchs. Emperor Tian Qi (reigned between 1620 and 1627) often played hide-and-seek with his attendants here.

金殿　乾清宫丹陛下东、西各有一座石台，东台上置江山金殿，西台上置社稷金殿，寓示皇帝坐镇江山，一统天下。

Gilded Pavilion　There is a gilded pavilion on either side of the marble terrace before the Palace of Heavenly Purity. The one on the east is called Jiangshan (Country) Pavilion; the one on the west is called Sheji (Government) Pavilion.

乾清宫内景 方形地平床上设金漆雕龙宝座和屏风,其上悬"正大光明"横匾,这是清代自雍正皇帝(1722～1735年在位)以后,在位皇帝为避免皇子间争夺皇位继承权而秘藏立储遗诏之处。

Inside the Palace of Heavenly Purity In the center of the main hall there is a square platform with a throne and an ornate dragon screen, both of which are gold painted and decorated with delicate carvings. High up in the middle of the hall there is a plaque with an inscription which reads "Be open and aboveboard". The emperors of the Qing Dynasty after Emperor Yong Zheng would write the name of his successor, put the paper in a box and hide the box behind the plaque. The box was opened when the emperor died, thus avoiding competition among his sons.

宝座靠背上的龙头　　Dragon head above the back

宝座扶手　　Handles

宝座靠背　　　　Back

宝座底座　　Seat

乾清宫宝座局部　　Details of the Golden Throne.

交泰殿 位于乾清宫与坤宁宫之间,规制如中和殿。殿名寓意天地交泰,帝后和睦。皇后逢大典及生日,在此受贺。每年仲春,后妃们在此殿举行亲蚕仪式。

Hall of Union (Jiaotaidian) Located between the Palace of Heavenly Purity and the Palace of Earthly Tranquility, the interior of this hall is similar to that of the Hall of Middle Harmony. Its name means "Heaven and earth are united", symbolizing the harmonious relationship between the emperor and the empress. Birthday celebrations of the empress were held in this hall. In spring the empress presided a ceremony to begin the silkworm breeding season.

飞檐 中国古建筑常见的艺术形式,其特征是,屋的角檐上翘,宛如飞翼。常见于亭榭楼阁,庙宇宫殿等建筑物。图为交泰殿飞檐。

Flying Eaves A common sight of ancient buildings in China is long eaves turning high up. The picture shows the flying eaves of the Hall of Union.

铜壶滴漏　为中国古代计时器，俗称漏壶，由日天壶、夜天壶、平水壶、分水壶和受水壶五部分构成。此壶至今完好无损，为故宫珍品，现存交泰殿。

Water Clock　On the east side of the Hall of Union stands a clepsydra, a time-piece used in ancient China. It is composed of five bronze vessels, each has a small hole at the bottom. When the uppermost vessel is filled with water, it begins to drip evenly through the holes.

自鸣钟　置于交泰殿内西侧,清嘉庆年间 (1796—1820年)制造。钟分上、中、下三层, 高5.6米,以罗马数字标记时数,先报刻、后 报时,声音宏亮,深达内宫。

Chiming Clock　Built during the reign of Emperor Jia Qing (1796-1820), the clock of three tiers is 5.6 meters high. The 12 figures on the dial are Roman numerials. The chiming could reach every corner of the Inner Court.

玺 图中地平床两边和宝座二面均为存放的宝玺。玺，即印，本为统称，自秦（前221—前206年）以后，专指皇帝之印。交泰殿内存有乾隆年间鉴定的宝玺25方。取二十五之数，源于《周易》"天数二十有五"之说，似有祈求上苍保佑"大清得享号二十有五"之意，清进关后实传十代而告终。

Imperial Seals Twenty-five imperial seals of the Qing emperors are kept in the Hall of Union. Emperor Qian Long hoped that by keeping 25 seals, the Qing Dynasty could rule the country for at least 25 generations. Nevertheless, his prayers did not work. The Qing Dynasty was overthrown on the 12th generation.

玉玺 宝玺之质有金、玉、檀香木之分，以玉居多，如图。此玉玺纽为蛟龙，以示皇权独尊。

Imperial Seals The 25 imperial seals are made of gold, jade or sandalwood. The jade seal in the picture has a handle in the shape of dragon.

坤宁宫 为明、清两代皇后的寝宫。1644年农民军领袖李自成率兵攻入北京，崇祯皇帝（1627—1644年在位）的周皇后自尽于宫里。清代自雍正以后，皇帝由乾清宫迁往养心殿居住，皇后也由此宫移居体顺堂。

Palace of Earthly Tranquility (Kunninggong)　It was the residence of the empress during the Ming and Qing times. In 1644 when the peasant uprising leader Li Zicheng seized Beijing, Empress Zhou of Emperor Chong Zhen (1627-1644) committed suicide here. After Yong Zheng, the Qing emperors moved their residence to the Hall of Cultivating the Mind and the empresses moved their residence to the Hall of Physical Harmony.

坤宁宫内景 中国满族礼重祀神，凡祭必于正寝。清顺治十二年（1655年）袭盛京清宁宫旧俗，将坤宁宫中部四间大堂改为萨满教祭神场所。祭礼分日祭、月祭、春秋大祭等，大祭之日帝、后临场。图中宝座为皇帝祭神时吃祭肉的座位。

Inside the Palace of Earthly Tranquility   The ruling class of the Qing Dynasty attached great importance to worshipping the God of Rites. In 1655 Emperor Shun Zhi turned four halls of this palace into a shrine for Shaman gods. Sacrificial ceremonies were held here in honor of the Sun, the Moon, in spring and autumn. The emperor and empress came in person. The throne in the picture was for the emperor to sit on when he ate the sacrificial meat.

大婚洞房　坤宁宫按满族风俗改建后,殿东两间暖阁为皇帝大婚洞房,婚后帝、后仅在此住两夜,第三天皇帝回养心殿,皇后回体顺堂。今阁内陈设保留光绪皇帝(1874～1908 年在位)大婚原状。

Bridal Chamber　After the renovation of the Palace of Earthly Tranquility according to Manchu's customs the anteroom to the east of the main hall became the bridal chamber. The emperor and empress would stay in this place for two nights after the wedding. Then the emperor went to live in the Hall of Mental Cultivation and the empress went to stay in the Hall of Physical Harmony. The bridal chamber has preserved the same decoration as used at the wedding of Emperor Guang Xu.

"开门见喜" 洞房内竖一木质朱漆曲尺形影壁,正中有大"囍"金字,四角为龙凤相拥的"囍"贴金图案,取帝、后合卺之意,人们把这叫作"开门见喜"。

'Doorstep Happiness' When entering the bridal chamber one first sees a red wooden screen wall. At its center is a large sign of double-happiness covered with gold leaf, and in its four corners are patterns of a dragon and a phoenix embracing each other, symbolizing the happy marriage of the emperor and empress.

煮肉灶房 设于坤宁宫东次间。每年祭神宰猪约1300头,图中三口大锅即为煮肉而设,青花瓷缸用于盛酒。

Meat Cooking Kitchen The kitchen on the east of the Palace of Earthly Tranquility would slaughter 1,300 pigs a year for sacrificial rites. The three giant cauldrons in the picture were used to cook the meat. The porcelain jar was filled with wine.

龙凤喜床 为一落地大木炕，床楣上挂"日升月恒"匾，
意为皇帝如旭日初升，皇后似上弦之月。

Dragon-Phoenix Bed The bed in the bridal chamber is
sheltered by a wooden structure. Over the front of the bed
is hung a plaque with an inscription, which reads "The
sun at dawn and the moon at the first quarter", referring
to the emperor and the empress.

百子帐 喜床悬挂特制的大红缎绣龙凤百子图幔帐，帐上婴童百态，童趣横生，象征皇帝子嗣昌盛，基业兴旺。

Hundred-Baby Drapery A drapery over the entire bridal bed is made of red satin and embroidered with the design of dragons, phoenixes and a hundred young boys in various postures, sybmolizing the fertility of the imperial family.

御花园 东西长130米,南北宽90米,它以主体建筑钦安殿为中心,左右对称,前后呼应。园内分布着10多座亭台楼阁,间有山石树木、花池盆景和五色石子甬道,是一处宫廷式花园。

Imperial Garden   The Imperial Garden is 130 meters long from east to west and 90 meters wide from south to north. Centering around the Hall of Imperial Peace, the garden has over 10 pavilions, terraces and towers and is beautifully embellished with fantastic rockeries, ancient cypress trees, bamboo groves and exotic flowering plants. A pathway is paved with pebbles of various colors.

古柏枝 御花园古柏大多繁枝交错，展延盘曲。图中柏枝犹如猕猴攀树，引人生趣。

Ancient Trees A dozen pine and cypress trees in the Imperial Garden are over 400 years old. The branches of the cypress tree in the picture look like monkeys climbing a tree.

连理柏 实为异干异根、距今已有400余年的两株古柏，柏枝纽结纠缠，树干相依相偎，颇似恋人幽会，其情缠绵，故称连理柏。

Twin Cypress Trees The two trees with their branches entwined look like two lovers embracing. They are more than 400 years old.

香炉　为故宫第一炉,高 4 米,炉身有六个"二龙戏珠"的火焰喷门,底座铸"三狮戏珠"浮图。它与"北京三绝"之一的雍和宫香炉齐名。

Incense Burner　This largest bronze incense burner in the Palace Museum is four meters high. The six smoke outlets are in the shape of two dragons playing a ball. A relief design on the bottom depicts three lions playing a ball.

天一门 为水磨砖砌的单元券门，是钦安殿正门，明代
称"天一之门"，取"天一生水"之意。门前置獬豸一对，
此兽为传说中的异兽，能辨曲直，置于门前，意在彰善惩
恶，弘扬光明。

Tianyi Gate　The single opening gate is the main entrance to the Hall of Imperial Peace. In front of the Tianyi
Gate are two gilt "Xiezhi". The mythical animal is believed to have the power to discern between right and
wrong.

"诸葛亮拜北斗星石" 位于天一门西侧。石面有天然生成的人形斑纹，其形头戴纶巾，身着紫袍，双手拱起，躬身下拜，前方点点星斗，颇似蜀汉政治家诸葛亮（公元181－234年）拜天之状，故名。

Zhuge Liang Worshipping the Big Dipper Zhuge Liang (181-234) was a great strategist. A rockery at the west side of Tianyi Gate resembles him in a silk headdress and a purple gown, bowing with both hands clasped in front seeming to worship the stars in the sky.

钦安殿　御花园内最大的宗教建筑,内奉水神玄武,供奉此神,意在宫中避火消灾。

The Hall of Imperial Peace (Qin'andian)　Inside the hall stands the statue of the King of Xuan Wu flanked by bronze statues, who was believed to be the Water God and could, therefore, prevent the palace buildings from catching fire.

焚帛炉 位于钦安殿西侧，用琉璃砖镶砌而成，是祭祀玄武神后用来焚烧祝版（祭文）、祝帛（绸幅祭文）的窑炉。

Memorial Paper Burner The glazed-tile furnace to the west of the Hall of Imperial Peace was used to burn sacrificial papers and silk scrolls to the King of Xuan Wu.

御景亭 建于由太湖石叠起的堆秀山顶，山的匾额"堆秀"、"云根"为乾隆皇帝御笔。每年九月九日重阳节，帝、后们登山入亭，了望紫禁城内外景色。

Imperial Sight Pavilion (Yujingting) The pavilion stands on an artificial hill of rocks from Taihu Lake. The inscriptions on two boards — "Collecting Excellence" and "Cloud Roots" — are in the handwriting of Emperor Qian Long. On the 9th day of the 9th lunar month the emperor and his consorts would ascend this height and enjoy the scenic beauty both within and outside the Imperial Palace.

四神祠 是皇帝祭祀代表东、西、南、北的青龙、白虎、朱雀、玄武四神的地方，以此表示皇帝承天命统御四方。

Four Gods Shrine The Four Gods, the Blue Dragon, White Tiger, Red Bird and King of Xuan Wu, represent four directions on the earth. The emperor paid homage to them meaning he ruled the world.

绛雪轩 "轩"是中国古建筑中带窗槛的小屋。绛雪轩平面呈"凸"字形,窗格用木条别出心裁地拼接出汉字"万寿无疆"图形。轩前原植海棠数株,海棠花初放殷红,落花时节白如雪,故名"绛雪轩"。

House of Crimson Snow (Jiangxuexuan) The lattice work of the windows is characterized by four Chinese characters meaning "Longevity". In front of it are some crabapple trees. Their white flowers look like snow, hence the name of the house.

万春亭 亭为上圆下方四出抱厦，含有古人朴素的宇宙观"天圆地方"之意。亭内原供奉蜀汉名将关羽(？—公元220年)牌位。

Pavilion of 10,000 Springs (Wanchunting) The structure is round above and square below, for people in ancient China believed heaven was round and earth was square. It used to serve as a shrine where a portrait of Guan Yu was worshipped.

83

浮碧亭 横跨于单孔石桥上,四面开敞,前出抱厦。桥下为一方形鱼池,池中春水碧绿,亭浮其上,故名浮碧亭。

Pavilion of Floating Green (Fubiting) The pavilion stands on a single-arch bridge of stone. Fish swim in a square pool of clear water under it.

金鱼戏睡莲 浮碧亭下鱼池中睡莲花开,金鱼嬉戏其间,一静一动,绿肥红瘦,相映成趣。

Goldfish and Water Lilies It is a wonderful sight in summer when water lilies under the Pavilion of Floating Green are in blossom and goldfish swim among them.

摛藻堂 位于御花园东北角,坐北朝南,背山临水,为乾隆皇帝读书和珍藏秘籍之所。堂中所藏《四库荟要》,为《四库全书》精萃之集。

Chicao Hall It is located at the northeastern corner of the Imperial Garden and faces south. It was built under the reign of Emperor Qian Long to house the encyclopedia The *Siku Quanshu (Complete Library of the Four Treasures of Knowledge)*, a famous collection of Chinese ancient books.

养性斋 清乾隆年间,皇家将全国所搜典籍存放斋中。末代皇帝溥仪(1906～1967年)曾在此师从英国人庄士敦学习英文。

Studio for Cultivating Nature (Yangxinzhai) During the reign of Emperor Qian Long, it served as a library where books collected from all over the country were kept. Fu Yi(1906 – 1967), the last emperor of China, was taught English here.

千秋亭 与万春亭相对应，二者形制雷同，仅藻井有细微差别。明嘉靖年间（1522—1566 年）改建成供佛庙宇。清代曾在此供奉同治皇帝（1861—1874 年在位）牌位。

Pavilion of 1,000 Autumns (Qianqiuting) Located opposite the Pavilion of 10,000 Springs and much similar in structure, the place served as a shrine during the reign of Emperor Jia Jing (1522-1566) of the Ming Dynasty. During the Qing Dynasty, the portrait of Emperor Tong Zhi (1861-1874) was worshipped in this place.

澄瑞亭 其建制如浮碧亭,原四面开门窗,为道教殿宇,现为四面透空的敞亭。

Pavilion of Pure Felicity (Chengruiting) The pavilion, similar in structure to the Pavilion of Floating Green, used to be a Daoist Shrine.

延晖阁 为清代选秀女处。按清制,每三年选秀女一次,应选女子由神武门入紫禁城,至延晖阁接受挑选。

Pavilion of Lasting Splendor (Yanhuige) During the Qing Dynasty palace maids were selected every three years. The candidates were examined in this place.

甬道 御花园的甬道为精选的各色鹅卵石铺就，其图案多以民间传说或典故为内容。图中路面的图案是"泼妇罚夫"，质朴逼真的人物造型把刁妇克夫的情景表现得惟妙惟肖，观之令人忍俊不禁。

Cobbled Pathway The pathway is paved with tiny cobble stones of various colors. The designs are rich and colorful, and cover a wide range of subjects. One picture is "Henpecked Husbands", which depicts two henpecked husbands kneeling on a wash board, being beaten by their wives.

铜路灯　紫禁城使用电灯始于光绪十四年（1888 年），在此之前，宫中街巷照明多用此种灯。

Bronze Road Lamp　The Imperial Palace began to use electric light in 1888. Before that bronze road lamps were used.

神武门　为故宫北门,高 31 米。皇后、妃嫔们前往蚕坛举行亲蚕仪式出入此门。崇祯皇帝出此门逃往煤山,吊死在槐树下。

Gate of Divine Prowess (Shenwumen)　The north gate to the Imperial Palace is 31 meters high. The empress and imperial concubines left the palace through this gate to attend the ceremony of starting silkworm breeding season. Cong Zhen, the last emperor of the Ming Dynasty, went through this gate to hang himself on a tree at Coal Hill.

前朝两翼区

前朝两翼区包括文华殿、武英殿两组建筑群。它们分列前朝三大殿左右,彼此呼应,东西对称,构成前朝格局。

文华殿为明清两代经筵典礼之地;武英殿明初为斋戒之所,清代康熙年间为宫廷刻书处。这两组建筑群整体布局十分简洁,结构颇为紧凑。在空间处理上,重点突出,主从明晰,谐调得当。两处环境清幽雅静,流水潺潺,古槐成荫,呈现出一派婉约清丽的园林气氛。

Two Wings of the Outer Court

The Outer Court is flanked by two groups of buildings represented by the Hall of Literary Glory on the east and the Hall of Military Excellence on the west.

The Hall of Lierary Glory was where Lecture/Banquet ceremonies were held; the Hall of Military Excellence was used by the emperor to fast in the early Ming Dynasty and by Emperor Kang Xi of the Qing Dynasty to prepare wood blocks for printing. The architectural characteristic of the buildings is simple and compact. The place is tranquil with tiny streams and ancient cypress trees.

文华殿 为前朝东翼主殿。皇帝在此斋居、举行经筵和召见文武大臣。

Hall of Literary Glory (Wenhuadian) The main building on the eastern wing of the Outer Court was used by the emperor as an abode for abstinence. Occasionally he would receive high officials here.

文渊阁 为皇家宫廷藏书处,《四库全书》、《古今图书集成》两部大百科全书即珍藏于此。

Pavilion of the Source of Literature (Wenyuange) It used to be the imperial library, housing the famous collection of *Siku Quanshu (Complete Library of the Four Treasures of Knowledge)* and the *Collected Works from the Past and Present*.

半间屋 中国古代计算房屋间数以两柱间距为一间,相距丈余。故宫殿堂楼阁人称九千九百九十九间半,这半间屋位于文渊阁西端,其两柱间距仅五尺左右。

Half Room In ancient China, the size of a house was measured by sections between pillars. A section between two pillars was called a "room", about three meters wide. The Imperial Palace has 9,999.5 rooms. The Half Room is located in the western part of the Pavilion of the Source of Literature.

箭亭 位于奉先殿南面广场中,为清代皇帝及子孙演习骑射之所。清皇室在奉先殿家庙前修建此亭,意在告诫子孙继承尚武精神,勿忘创业之艰。

Archery Pavilion (Jianting) It is situated in an open ground to the south of the Hall of Ancestral Worship. During the Qing Dynasty the open ground was for the emperor and his children to practice shooting and equestrian skills.

撷芳殿　俗称"南三所"，为皇子居所，建筑规格均为三进院落，殿顶覆绿色琉璃瓦，以象征新生。

Hall of Gathering Fragrance (Xiefangdian)　The residence for the Qing princes is composed of three courtyards with roofs of green glazed tiles.

东华门 为故宫东门,高33米。文武百官上朝或退值出入东、西华门。皇帝驾崩,灵柩由东华门出,故俗称"鬼门",因之门钉亦用阴数(偶数),计八行九列七十二个,以表生死有别。

East Flowery Gate (Donghuamen) It is the east gate of the Imperial Palace. The gate tower is 33 meters high. When officials went to court or came back from work, they always entered or left the Imperial Palace through this gate or West Flowery Gate. In the Qing Dynasty, the emperor's coffin was carried out of or into the palace through this gate, thus its nickname "the Gate of Ghost". Its 72 door knobs are even in number. This is because in the feudal society people believed that even numbers and the dead belonged to the same *Yin*.

门洞 图为东华门门洞，呈拱形，券长 24.95 米，底宽 4.92 米，高 6.78 米。步入其间，顶高道长，两壁森森，思古之情油然而生。

Door Passageway This passageway of East Flowery Gate is 24.95 meters long, 4.92 meters wide on the ground and 6.78 meters high. The gloomy darkness reminds visitors of the remote times.

下马碑 故宫为禁地，故在午门前、东西华门外的左右两侧均立有高约 4 米、宽 1 米的石碑，此处碑文为"至此下马"四字，举凡文武百官至碑前，均须落轿下马，徒步入宫。

Dismounting Tablets Two stone tablets, about four meters high, one meter wide, stand in front of West and East Flowery Gates. Each tablet is inscribed on both sides with "Dismount". Court officials had to get off their palanquins and horses on this spot, and then went into the palace on foot.

武英殿　为前朝西翼主殿，规制如文华殿。明代皇帝居此斋戒，召见大臣纵论国事，谈经讲学。明末李自成攻占北京，入此殿称帝。满清入关，顺治皇帝（1643—1661年在位）在此举行登基大典。

Hall of Martial Spirit (Wuyingdian)　The main hall on the west wing of the Outer Court is similar in structure to the Hall of Literary Glory. During the Ming Dynasty, it was used by the emperor for abstinancy and to give audience to high officials. In 1644 Li Zicheng, a peasant rebellion leader, overthrew the Ming Dynasty and proclaimed himself the emperor in this hall. Soon the Manchus took over Beijing and Emperor Shun Zhi (1643-1661) ascended the throne here.

东西六宫

东、西六宫分列于后三宫的东、西两侧。东六宫包括景仁宫、承乾宫、钟粹宫、延禧宫、永和宫和景阳宫。西六宫包括永寿宫、翊坤宫、储秀宫、太极殿、长春宫和咸福宫。

东、西六宫为明、清两代妃嫔居所，全部为深广各50米的庭院式建筑。每一庭院的主殿座落于主轴线上，东西配殿对称，左右耳房相配，构成"前朝后寝"的两进格局。前殿为房主会客议事之宫，后殿为寝卧颐养之室。东、西六宫四面有宫墙环绕，各庭院相对独立，但又互为依存，整体设计严谨有序，建筑规制大体统一，给人以虽有千门万户但又秩序井然之感。

Six Eastern Palaces and Six Western Palaces

The Six Eastern Palaces and Six Western Palaces are located on the two sides of the three rear palaces. The Six Eastern Palaces include Palace of Great Benevolence, Palace of Heavenly Inheritance, Palace of Quintessence, Palace of Prolonged Happiness, Palace of Eternal Harmony and Palace of Great Brilliance; and the Six West Palaces are Palace of Eternal Longevity, Palace of Assisting the Empress, Palace of Gathering Elegance, Hall of Supremacy, Palace of Eternal Spring and Palace of Universal Happiness. They were the residences of imperial concubines. With a surrounding wall each palace forms a compound of 2,500 square meters. The main halls stand in the middle and the side-chambers are in the east and west. The hall in the front yard was used for formal audience, and the hall in the back-yard served as the bed-chamber. The architecture of the 12 palaces are much similar, and they are connected by passageways.

斋宫 是皇帝祭天、祈谷前斋戒、沐浴的寝宫。按典制规定，祭天前三天，皇帝必须到斋宫独宿三昼夜，此间不食荤腥、不饮酒、不娱乐、不近女色、不理刑名，这就是所谓"斋戒"。此斋宫建于清雍正年间，称"内斋"，天坛斋宫称"外斋"。图为斋宫宫门。

Palace of Abstinence (Zhaigong) The ancient tradition required the emperors of both Ming and Qing dynasties to worship Heaven and pray for good harvest in the Temple of Heaven on winter solstice. Three days before the event, the emperor had to stay in the Palace of Abstinence, where he was supposed to eat no meat, have no contact with women, drink no wine, have no merry-making and be concerned with no legal matters. This palace was built during the reign of Qing Empeor Yong Zheng (1723-1735).

诚肃殿　为斋宫主殿,抱厦檐下悬"斋宫"匾额。正厅有"敬天"牌匾,以表皇帝敬天之心专一致诚;卧室挂"敬止"警语,警示皇帝不要有非份之想。

Hall of Sincerity (Chengsudian)　Above the eave of this main hall of Palace of Abstinence hangs a board with the inscription of "Palace of Abstinence". The inscription on the plaque in the hall reads "Respectful to Heaven". A motto in the bed-chamber reads " Restrain One's Desires".

奉先殿　为中国封建社会的五坛八庙之一,类似皇家供奉列祖列宗的太庙。所不同的是,这里不仅供奉先帝先后灵位,未作过皇帝的先祖亦可在此供奉,以展后辈"孝思之诚"。此殿现为钟表馆,内展近代各式钟表共 182 件。

Hall of Ancestral Worship (Fengxiandian)　It was one of the Five Imperial Shrines and Eight Temples in ancient China. This hall in the Imperial Palace functioned as the ancestral shrine of the royal family. It is now an exhibition room displaying 182 pieces of clocks and watches.

宫墙 故宫东、西六宫街巷纵横，宫墙幽深，人行其间，仅观一线天，颇有与世隔绝、阴森冷漠之感。

Palace Wall The Six Eastern Palaces and Six Western Palaces are crisscrossed with narrow passageways between high palace walls. They are so narrow one feels squeezed in.

景仁宫 东六宫之一，妃嫔住所。清末光绪皇帝的宠妃珍妃曾在此居住，珍妃死后，人去楼空。

Palace of Great Benevolence (Jingrengong) A favorite concubine, Zhenfei, of Emperor Guang Xu (1874-1908), once lived here. After she was murdered by the empress dowager, the palace remained vancant for a long time.

承乾宫 位于景仁宫北。明末为崇祯皇帝 (1627—1644 年在位)的田贵妃的寝宫；清代 顺治皇帝的宠妃董鄂氏亦居此宫。此后有多 位妃嫔入住。

Palace of Heavenly Inheritance (Chengqiangong) Lady Tian, a favorite concubine of Emperor Chong Zhen, and a favorite concubine of Emperor Shun Zhi, once lived in this palace.

钟粹宫 原名咸阳宫，为皇太子寝宫，明隆庆 年间(1567—1572 年)改为钟粹宫。清末为光 绪皇帝的隆裕皇后居住；宣统皇帝初入宫时， 曾居于此。

Palace of Quintessence (Zhongcuigong) It was originally named Xianyang and served as the residence of the crown prince. The present name was given between 1567 and 1572. Empress Long Yu of Emperor Guang Xu and the child emperor Xuan Tong once stayed in this palace.

永和宫 东六宫之一。明代为贵妃居所,清代光绪年间瑾妃居于此宫。

Palace of Eternal Harmony (Yonghe-gong) One of the Six Eastern Palaces, it was a residence of imperial concubines. Imperial Consort Ji of Emperor Guang Xu once lived here.

迎瑞门 此门与昌祺门相对,构成东西夹道,此夹道又贯穿南北通道,形成四通八达的格局。

Gate of Ushering in Goodness (Ying-ruimen) A passageway runs between this gate and Changqi Gate to link up a south-north passageway.

景阳宫 明代神宗皇帝（1572~1620 年在位）的孝靖皇后曾居此。康熙二十五年（1686 年）曾重修，为藏书之所。后殿曰"御书房"，康熙为皇子时，曾在此宫读书。

Palace of Great Brilliance（Jingyanggong） Empress Xiaojing of Emperor Shen Zong（1572 – 1620）of the Ming Dynasty once lived here. The palace was rebuilt in 1686 during the Qing Dynasty. The rear hall served as the Imperial Study. When Emperor Kang Xi was crown prince he took his lessons here.

影壁　为中国古建筑特征之一。举凡院落，多在大门外设一影壁，既可作该院落的屏障，以别内外；又可装饰门面，以显房主的阔绰与气派。此影壁名为鸳鸯戏水，寓意帝、后恩爱相随。

Screen Wall　Screen wall could be seen behind the front gate of almost all large residences in old China. It served as decoration and a screen hiding the interior of the compound from passers-by. The design of this screen wall is "Mandarin Ducks Playing on Water", symbolizing harmonious relations between the emperor and his empress.

西六宫鸟瞰　　Bird's-eye view of the Six Western Palaces.

影壁"盒子"　影壁上的装饰图案或艺术造型多集中于壁身中心和四角,中心称为"盒子",四角叫作"岔角"。此"盒子"的画面为一对鸳鸯,它们形影不离,嬉戏于莲花丛中,形象生动、情韵深长。

Screen Wall Center　Most screen walls have decorative patterns in the center and four corners. The mandarin ducks swim amidst lotus flowers is a representing theme of the center design of screen walls.

养心门 即养心殿的大门，庑殿式门楼，楼顶及左右"八"字影壁均镶嵌着琉璃构件，整个门面端庄典雅，华贵气派。

Gate of Mental Cultivation (Yangxinmen)
The main entrance to the Hall of Mental Cultivation has a gate tower. The screen walls flanking it are decorated with patterns of glazed tiles.

玉璧　设置于养心门外。玉璧为圆形，正中有孔，玉面碧绿青润，质地纯净。镶嵌玉璧的方形架精雕腾龙流云图案，其工艺精湛，形象生动。将玉璧设置于养心殿大门外，更显示皇家要地的富贵庄严之气，凌然轩昂之势。

Jade　The round jade piece placed outside the Gate of Mental Cultivation is emerald in color and has a square hole in the center. The frame holding the jade has carvings of dragon-cloud design. This magnificent ornament enhanced the solemn atmosphere.

养心殿 建于明代，清雍正时重修。殿内陈设讲究，是雍正皇帝以后历代皇帝处理政务的地方。每天清晨，皇帝在此接见军机大臣，听取政务。慈禧太后揽权期间所谓"垂帘听政"就在这里。

Hall of Mental Cultivation (Yangxindian) The hall was first built in the Ming Dynasty and rebuilt under the reign of Yong Zheng of the Qing Dynasty. The Qing emperors after Yong Zheng all handled state affairs here. Every morning they would receive important ministers in this hall. Empress Dowager Ci Xi ruled China behind the certain in this hall.

养心殿大堂　堂内设宝座，上悬"中正仁和"匾，为雍正皇帝御题。这里即是百官"陛见"之处。

Inside the Hall of Mental Cultivation　In the main room of the front hall hangs a horizontal board bearing the Chinese characters for "Just and Benevolent" in Emperor Yong Zheng's handwriting. This is where the emperor gave audience to his ministers.

养心殿东暖阁　这里是"辛酉政变"后慈禧、慈安两太后"垂帘听政"处。黄色纱帘前后设两个宝座，小皇帝坐前面，仅作摆设，一切军政大事均由帘内太后决定。六岁的同治皇帝和四岁的光绪皇帝先后在此充当傀儡。

East Warm Chamber　After the 1861 Coup Empress Dowagers Ci Xi and Ci An took over the power and began to "hold court behind the certain". The 6-year-old child emperor, Tong Zhi was seated on the throne in front, while the two empress dowagers were seated on the large throne behind. There was a yellow gauze curtain between the two thrones.

象驮宝瓶 为宝座前饰物。"象"寓意太平，象驮宝瓶，瓶内装五谷，表示五谷丰登，吉庆有余，故称"太平有象"。

Elephant and Precious Bottle The sculpture is placed in front the throne. The elephant was a symbol of "peace". The precious bottle on its back was filled with grains to symbolize good harvest.

皇帝寝宫 图为寝宫外间，隔扇内为皇帝卧室。清代自雍正皇帝以后，历代皇帝均居于此。室内"天行健"、"自强不息"匾额均为光绪皇帝手笔。

Bedroom of the Emperor The bedroom behind the screen was for all the Qing emperors after Yong Zheng. The two inscriptions on the horizontal boards in Emperor Guang Xu's handwriting read: "Follow the Heavenly Law" and "Self Reliant".

龙床 皇帝自诩"真龙天子"，其卧床称为"龙床"。床楣所悬"又日新"匾为慈禧太后所书，其意为保持德行日贤于一日。

Dragon Bed The emperor claimed he was the dragon. So his bed was called dragon bed. The inscription above the bed is in the handwriting of Empress Dowager Ci Xi, meaning to retain virtue.

三希堂　为养心殿西暖阁的一间小房,乾隆皇帝将中国历史上著名的书法家王羲之(公元303—361年)的《快雪时晴帖》,王献之(公元344—386年)的《中秋帖》和王珣(公元350～401年)的《伯远帖》三件希世珍宝藏于此,故名"三希堂"。

Room of Three Rarities (Sanxitang)　It is a room of the West Warm Chamber of the Hall of Mental Cultivation. Emperor Qian Long kept three samples of calligraphy by Wang Xizhi (303-361), Wang Xianzhi (344-386) and Wan Xun (350-401), famous calligraphers of the Jin Dynasty (265-420) in this room.

水晶石　置于养心殿后部体顺堂院中,此石晶莹剔透,纯洁无瑕。用它点缀皇后居住的庭院,似有喻示皇后光明磊落、心地坦荡之意。

Crystal　This impect piece of crystal decorates the courtyard of the Hall of Physical Harmony behind the Hall of Mental Cultivation. It was for reminding the empress to be honest and upright.

嘉祉门——纯祐门夹道　为西六宫最南端的东西向横街，向东可达内廷，向西可出宫门。

Passageway between Jiazhi Gate and Chunyou Gate
This is the southernmost alley of the Six Western Palaces.
To its east is the Inner Court; to its west is an exit of the
Imperial Palace.

永寿宫 位于西六宫东南角,妃嫔居所。明代宦官魏忠贤专横跋扈,曾居住过此宫,并将宫内敞院作为蹴鞠之地。

Palace of Eternal Longevity (Yongshougong) The residence of imperial concubines at the southeastern corner of the Six Western Palaces was once occupied by the tyrant Eunuch Wei Zhongxian of the Ming Dynasty. He played football in the courtyard.

翊坤宫 与东六宫的承乾宫相对称,向为妃嫔居所。慈禧太后为贵妃时曾居此宫。

Palace of Assisting the Empress (Yikungong) It is located on the opposite side of the Palace of Heavenly Inheritance of the Six Eastern Palaces. Empress Dowager Ci Xi lived here when she was still an imperial concubine.

木影壁　故宫东西六宫每组院落大都有一影壁，此为明、清宫殿建筑定制。影壁多为木制，上书吉祥语。图中影壁位于翊坤宫院内。

Wooden Screen Wall　In every compound of the Six Eastern and Six Western Palaces there is a wooden screen wall inscribed with auspicious words. This is the wooden screen in the compound of the Palace of Assisting the Empress.

凤凰 中国民间传说中的神鸟，雄为凤，雌为凰，通称凤凰，其形为鸡头、蛇颈、燕颔、龟背、鱼尾，五彩色，高六尺许。宫中凤凰被神话为皇后化身。图中凤凰为铜制，翊坤宫和长春宫前均有陈设。

Phoenix The phoenix in Chinese legend is a divine bird. Its first half looks like that of a swan goose and its latter half looks like that of a Chinese unicorn. Its plume has all the five colors. The 2-meter-high bronze phoenix in the picture is seen in the Palace of Assisting the Empress and the Palace of Lasting Spring.

体和殿 康熙年间由储秀门拆建而成。光绪皇帝的珍妃在此入选。慈禧太后住储秀宫时在此殿用膳,每餐主食 50 多种,菜 120 余样,用肉 500 多斤,鸡鸭 100 余只,由 450 人前后侍候。

Hall of Displaying Harmony (Tihedian) It was built on the site of the Gate of Gathering Excellence which was torn down during the reign of Emperor Kang Xi. Zhenfei was chosen as an imperial concubine of Emperor Guang Xu in this hall. When Empress Dowager Ci Xi stayed in the Palace of Gathering Elegance she had her meals in this hall. One dinner was made up with 50 kinds of staple food and 120 dishes, consuming 250 kilograms of meat and 100 chickens and ducks. She was attended by 450 people at

储秀宫 西六宫之一,与东六宫的钟粹宫相对称。慈禧太后发迹前曾以贵人身份入住后殿,并在此生下同治皇帝。她五十大寿时,在储秀、体和、翊坤等处举行盛大庆典,耗资甚巨。民国初年,溥仪的皇后婉容曾入居此宫。

Palace of Gathering Elegance (Chuxiugong) One of the Six Western Palaces, it stands opposite the Palace of Quintessence across the central axis. Empress Dowager Ci Xi moved to live here after she was promoted to Ladyship and gave birth to the future Emperor Tong Zhi. A grand ceremony was held here on her 50th birthday. In the early Republic the dethroned emperor Pu Yi and his wife Wan Rong once lived in this palace.

铜龙　龙为中国古代传说中有鳞有须并能兴风作雨的神兽，与麟、凤、龟并称"四灵"。中国历代帝王皆以龙自诩，世称"真龙天子"。图中铜龙设于妃嫔居住的储秀宫前，疑是慈禧太后谕制。

Bronze Dragon　In Chinese legend there are four divine animals: unicorn, phoenix, turtle and dragon. The dragon could invoke wind and rain. Emperors in China likened themselves the dragon. The bronze dragon in the picture is placed in the Palace of Gathering Elegance. It is believed it was made at the order of Empress Dowager Ci Xi.

"万寿无疆"赋 刻于储秀宫东侧廊壁，是慈禧太后生日时两位大臣作的恭维词赋。

"Eulogy of Longevity" It was composed by two scholars for the birthday of Empress Dowager Ci Xi and inscribed on the wall to the east of the Palace of Gathering Elegance.

宝座　设于储秀宫内，是慈禧太后召见大臣，议论国事的地方。

Throne　Empress Dowager sat on this throne in the Palace of Gathering Elegance to receive court ministers.

八方罩　所谓罩，实为用以分割房屋空间的屏障，其形式有栏杆罩、落地罩、花罩、炕罩等。故宫种类繁多的罩多用名贵花梨木、楠木制作，罩上透雕缠枝花卉或吉祥鸟兽，雕工精细，形象生动，犹如工艺品。

Partition Screens　Used to divide the space in a hall or room into private sections or placed on a platform bed as decoration, they come in various shapes. Most of them are made of precious pear and nanmu wood, and bear relief carvings of flowering plants, birds and animals.

慈禧太后"龙床"　床设檀木葫芦炕罩,其上透雕子孙万代图案。床上铺锦绣缎被,张挂三层苏绣幔帐,皆为五彩缎绸所作。如此奢华的床上陈设,在宫中仅此一处。

"Dragon Bed of Ci Xi"　On the bed is a screen of sandal-wood carved with many young boys. The quilts, mattresses and three layers of drapery are of colorful silk and satin. This bed is the most extravagantly decorated in the Imperial Palace.

象牙船　存放于储秀宫内,共两只,一为龙形,一为凤状。船长 91.5 厘米,宽 35 厘米,高 58 厘米,船上雕刻着福、禄、寿三星及群仙众神共 42 个人物,其形象逼真,活灵活现,堪称艺术精品。这两件珍宝是大臣们在千秋节恭奉给慈禧太后的礼品。

Ivory Boats　The Palace of Gathering Elegance has two ivory boats, one in the shape of a dragon and the other in the shape of a phoenix. Both are 91.5 centimeters long, 35 centimeters wide and 58 centimeters high. Forty-two immortals are carved on the boats. They were birthday presents of court ministers to Empress Dowager Ci Xi.

太极殿 中国古人谓"太极",有天宫、仙界的意思。以此作殿名,似有象征仙境、洪福齐天之意。清同治皇帝的瑜妃曾居住此殿。

Hall of Supremacy（Taijidian） "Supremacy" in ancient China meant the Heavenly Palace and Immortal Land. Lady Yu and Emperor Tong Zhi once lived in this place.

太极殿宝座 其两侧设有形如象的角端(传说中的神兽),寓示在位皇帝乃圣明之君。

Throne in the Hall of Supremacy Two Yiduan (a mythical animal) stand on either side of the throne, meaning the emperor was wise and upright.

从戏台看长春宫 宫名含有春光长驻之意。同治皇帝亲政后慈禧太后移居此宫；宣统皇帝的淑妃文绣亦曾居此。长春宫小戏台为慈禧太后谕旨由太极殿后殿和长春门改建而成，她五十大寿时，曾在此演戏相庆。

Palace of Eternal Spring (Changchungong) After Emperor Tong Zhi assumed the reins of government Empress Dowager Ci Xi moved to this palace. Emperor Xuan Tong and his concubine Wenxiu once lived here. A small open-air theater was built in the compound for the 50th birthday of Empress Dowager Ci Xi.

长春宫四合院　平面为正方形,其建筑为一正两厢、前后两进的四合院,与北京民间习见的四合院格局基本一致。

Compound of the Palace of Eternal Spring　The square compound is made up with two courtyards with a main house and two wings, much similar in design of ordinary courtyards in old Beijing.

长春宫游廊　廊壁遍绘工笔壁画，题材取自中国古典小说《红楼梦》，绘制于清光绪年间。此处壁画除具有较强的装饰效果外，还增加了游廊的纵深感。

Corridor of the Palace of Eternal Spring　On the walls of a corridor is a mural "A Dream of Red Mansions", which was made under the reign of Emperor Guang Xu. The corridor was done in perspective to give the viewer an impression that the corridor is extending into far distance.

壁画片断 画面表现的是《红楼梦》女主人公之一史湘云设螃蟹宴,大观园群钗聚会咏菊花的场景。壁画因年代久远已显陈旧,但亭榭池水依稀可辨,人物形象仍楚楚动人,显示了绘画大师的高超技艺。

Detail of the Mural It depicts a crab banquet given by Shi Xiangyun, one of the beauties in "A Dream of Red Mansions". Though the paint has much faded through years, the human figures and landscape still show the skills of great masters.

长春宫宝座　东西六宫宝座多为缎面铺垫，木质雕椅，不似前朝宝座那般包金镶玉、奢华庄严，有较浓厚的生活气息，力图创造出一种恬适安逸、清静温馨的环境。

Throne in the Palace of Eternal Spring　Most of thrones in the Six Eastern and Western Palaces are made of wood and covered with a satin cushion, unlike those in the Outer Court that are gilded and elaborately carved.

妃嫔卧室 "深宫多幽怨，庭院何清冷"，多少妃嫔在此翘首以待皇帝的幸临！

Bedroom of Imperial Concubines The numerous concubines in the Imperial Palace spent most of their lives in bitter desolation.

远眺雨花阁　雨花阁为宫内最高佛堂,四条巨龙匍匐在四角攒尖的屋脊上,赫然醒目。阁分三层,上层供欢喜佛五尊,中层供康熙皇帝大成功德佛位,下层供西天番佛。

Pavilion of Raining Flowers (Yuhuage)　The tower at the top has a hipped roof covered with gilded bronze tiles with four gilded galloping dragons on the four ridges. Five Buddhist statues are placed on the top floor. The second floor houses a memorial image of Emperor Kang Xi and the ground floor has Buddhist statues from the Western Land.

宁寿全宫

宁寿全宫俗称"外东路",占地46000平方米,分前后两部分。前半部以皇极殿、宁寿宫为主,是太上皇接受群臣朝贺之处,为前朝。后半部分三路,正中一路以养性殿、乐寿堂为主;东有畅音阁和阅是楼一组燕乐建筑;西有乾隆花园。

宁寿全宫是乾隆皇帝当太上皇以后的颐养之所。但他在"归政仍训政"的名义下,仍大权在握,因此这里建筑处处体现出与中轴线的主体建筑相仿,规制极高。步入此地,殿廷辉煌,装饰华丽,各种稀世珍宝璀璨夺目,奇花异卉多姿多彩,令人流连忘返。

Outer Eastern Palaces

The Outer Eastern Palaces of 46,000 square meters were specially built for the retired Emperor Qian Long of the Qing Dynasty. This group of buildings is independent of the other parts of the Imperial Palace; however the general plan is made exactly after that on the central axis, i. e. three big halls in the Outer Court and three palaces in the Inner Court. The Outer Court in the south was where the retired Emperor Qian Long received festive greetings from high-ranking officials. The Inner Court in the north was the residence of the retired emperor and his empress.

皇极门 为宁寿全宫正门,门为三洞七楼,琉璃花顶,色彩缤纷,不惧火烧,不畏风霜,堪称故宫诸琉璃花门之首。

Gate of Imperial Supremacy (Huangjimen) The main entrance to the Outer Eastern Palaces has three openings and seven gate towers with glazed tile roofs. It is called Flowery Gate because the glazed tiles are of various colors.

九龙壁 是清代现存三座九龙壁之一，位于皇极门前。壁高3.5米，宽29.4米，由270块彩色琉璃件构成。壁面九龙姿态各异，飞腾嬉戏于海涛云气之中，颇有呼之欲出的感觉。

Nine-Dragon Screen Three Nine-Dragon Screens of the Qing Dynasty have been left in China. This one in the Outer Eastern Palaces is 3.5 meters high, 29.4 meters long and built with 270 glazed multi-colored tiles. Nine dragons romp in the sea against a background of waves, cliffs and clouds.

宁寿门　为五楹庑殿式宫门，坐北朝南，门前一对鎏金铜狮镇守左右。秉门正看，它黄琉璃瓦覆顶，下承白石须弥座，雕梁画栋，沥粉贴金，门两侧为琉璃看墙的"八"字影壁，其建筑规制有如内廷乾清门。

Gate of Tranquil Longevity (Ningshoumen)　The gate is much like a palace hall with a roof of yellow glazed tiles, marble foundation, pillars with picture paintings. Two gilded bronze lions stand on either side. The wall spreading from the gate is covered with glazed tiles.

门钉 原为固定木板之用,以后逐渐演变成含有等级差别的装饰。故宫除东华门外,所有大门均用九行九列门钉,因中国古人把"九"视为"阳极数",是至尊之数,所以皇家器物多用"九"。

Door Knobs In ancient China people believed nine was the largest number and thus the most important. The emperor represented the highest power. So all the gates of the Imperial Palace, except the East Flowery Gate, have 81 door knobs in nine rows, each of nine knobs.

镀金铜狮 置于宁寿门左右两侧。铜狮通体贴金,铸造精美,形象极为生动。

Gilded Bronze Lion Two gilded bronze lions stand on either side of the Gate of Tranquil Longevity.

皇极殿 大殿居中当阳,为太上皇临朝正殿。它重檐庑殿顶,青白石须弥座,丹楹琐窗,金琢墨彩画,一如大内正衙太和殿规制。此殿现为珍宝馆,内藏明清两代皇室珍宝。

Hall of Imperial Supremacy (Huangjidian) The main hall of the Palace of Tranquil Longevity was rebuilt for holding official ceremonies after Emperor Qian Long retired. The magnificent structure has a roof with double eaves, white stone foundation and painted beams. The entire building was modelled after the Hall of Supreme Harmony and the Palace of Heavenly Purity. Now it is an exhibition room for the treasures of the Ming and Qing dynasties.

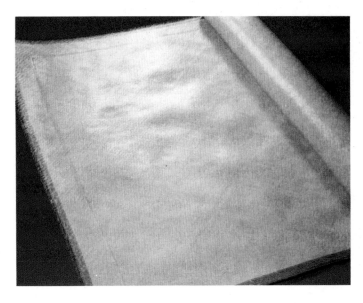

象牙席 属稀世珍宝。席长 216 厘米,宽 139 厘米。制做此席须精选象牙,并将象牙作特殊处理,然后劈成厚 0.1 厘米,宽 0.3 厘米的象牙条编织成席。清雍正年间曾制做五件,现存三件。

Ivory Mat It is 216 centimeters by 139 centimeters and woven of ivory filaments less than 0.3 centimeter wide and 0.1 centimeter thick. Five ivory mats were made during the reign of Yong Zheng. Three have remained.

"大禹治水"玉雕 是中国现存的最大玉雕,表现上古大禹治水的故事。成品高2.24米,重5吨。玉料出自新疆,运至扬州雕琢,琢成后运回北京,前后耗时十余年。

"Dayu Harnessing Floods" The largest piece of jade carving in China today, it is 2.24 meters high and weighs five tons. This huge block of jade was quarried in Xinjiang and transported to Yangzhou. After the carving was finished there it was shipped to Beijing. The whole process took ten years.

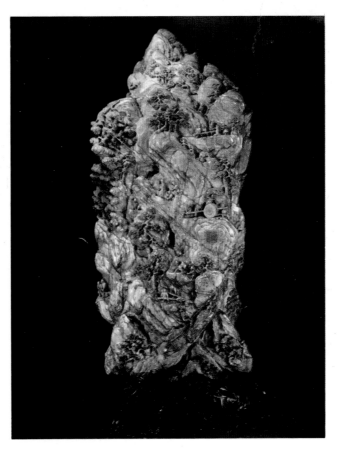

如意 初为搔痒工具,令人称心如意,因而得名。清代成为皇家宫殿重要的陈设品,宝座旁或寝宫案几上均摆一柄,以示吉祥。每逢新帝即位,王公大臣须向皇帝敬献如意;皇帝亦用如意赏赐臣属。遴选皇后,被选中者赐如意为证。

Ruyi In the early days, a ruyi was used as a back-scratcher. It became a symbol of good luck and ornament during the Qing Dynasty. On such festive occasions as the emperor's coronation or birthday, the princes and ministers would present ruyi to the emperor, empress or imperial concubines as a gift. It was an inevitable decoration in major halls and by the throne in the Imperial Palace. When the young emperor chose his wife, he would give a ruyi to the girl he liked best. The emperor also gave it to officials as a gift.

宁寿宫 制如坤宁宫。东间为卧室，西间是祭神之所，内有食肉时就坐的大木炕和跳神法器。慈禧太后每年腊月、正月均在此宫居住。

Palace of Tranquil Longevity (Ningshougong) The building was modelled after the Palace of Earthly Tranquility. The east anteroom was the bedroom and the west anteroom served as a shrine where there was a huge wooden coach and sacrificial objects. Empress Dowager Ci Xi would stay here in the last month of the lunar year and the beginning of the new year.

畅音阁　建于 1772 年，清代三大戏楼之一。它高 20.71 米，分上、中、下三层。下层天花板中心有天井与上层串通，二层戏台设有绞车，可巧设机关布景，上天入地，变幻无穷。戏台底部有窨井五眼，作为表演用水之源。

Pavilion of Fluent Music（Changyinge）

Built in 1772, it was one of three most famous theaters in the Qing Dynasty. The 21-meter-high structure has three stories. The lower floor has openings in the ceiling so actors could come down from the second floor through them. Under one of the five openings there is a water well, which can enhance the sound effects by resonance. A capstan was installed under every opening to lift the actors or the setting up to the first floor.

乾隆花园一角 花园共四进院落。园内庭院衔联，叠石为山，松竹布景，亭轩点染。人们漫步园中，步移景换，涉门成趣，其乐无穷。

Qian Long's Garden The garden is 160 meters long and 137 meters wide from east to west, and consists of four small courtyards. Artificial hills built with rocks are seen everywhere, and pines, cypresses and bamboo groves add great beauty to the garden.

古华轩 为五开间歇山卷棚式敞轩,轩前古楸曾死而复生,乾隆皇帝以为吉兆。每当春夏之交,楸树红花似锦,因汉字"花"与"华"音同义近,故取名古华轩。

House of Ancient Glory (Guhuaxuan) The pavilion has a gabled roof without walls. An old catalpa tree stands in front of it. Emperor Qian Long believed the tree would bring good luck to his offsprings because it was once dead and then revived. It blooms in late spring and early summer.

乾隆书匾 古华轩内悬挂着四块诗匾,均为乾隆皇帝赞美古楸及园内景色而作。

Inscriptions of Emperor Qian Long Emperor Qian Long wrote poems to praise the old catalpa tree. The poems were inscribed on four boards which were hung in the House of Ancient Glo-

禊赏亭流杯渠　渠深 10 厘米，作如意形环绕。每逢三月上巳节，人们将酒杯漂浮水面，宛转曲流，即所谓泛觞之乐。

Cup-Floating Canal in Xishang Pavilion　Wine cups would be floated along the winding 10-centimeter-deep canal cut into the rock floor during a festival held in the spring, meaning to cleanse away evil influences.

抄手游廊　中国的园林布景，凡重要庭院和大型建筑物之间，都在正门两侧及两厢设置廊，人称"抄手游廊"。其作用是连接建筑物和贯通走道，既可为主体建筑增辉，又可避雨雪。

Wing Corridor　Corridor is an important part of ancient gardening in China. Many mansions and high buildings also have corridors. Corridors flanking the front gate or along wing houses serve as passageways as well as an ornamental object.

承露台　相传汉武帝（前141－前85年在位）好神仙，作承露台，承接甘露，以为服之可延年。此台名"承露"，即隐含求仙之意。

Dew-Collecting Terrace　Emperor Wu Di（141-85 B. C.）yearned to become an immortal. He built dew-collecting terraces to collect dew to drink, believing the "heavenly water" could prolong his life. The tradition survived after several thousand years.

珍妃井　珍妃为光绪皇帝宠妃，因支持皇帝新政被打入冷宫。1900年八国联军攻入北京，慈禧太后外逃前令太监将其推入井中溺死，年仅二十五岁，此井因此得名。

Zhenfei's Well　Zhenfei was Emperor Guang Xu's favorite concubine, but she was on bad terms with Empress Dowager Ci Xi for she supported the 1898 Reform Movement. In 1900 the Allied Forces of Eight Powers invaded Beijing. Before her fleeing Ci Xi ordered an eunuch to push Zhenfei into the well and was drowned. Then she was only 25 years old.